Contents

Life in the sea

Jellyfish are not what they seem.
Do not let their name fool you.
Jellyfish are not fish at all!

Jellyfish are sea animals.
They float in seas and
oceans around the world.

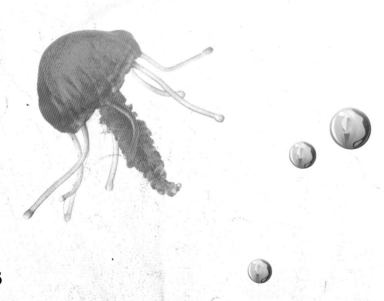

Up close

Jellyfish are many sizes.

Some are as small as a pea.

Others are bigger than a human.

They can be 2 metres wide.

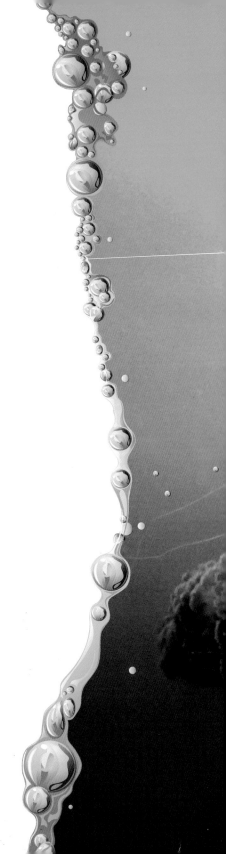

Bright colours cover some jellyfish.
Other jellyfish are clear.
Some jellyfish even glow!

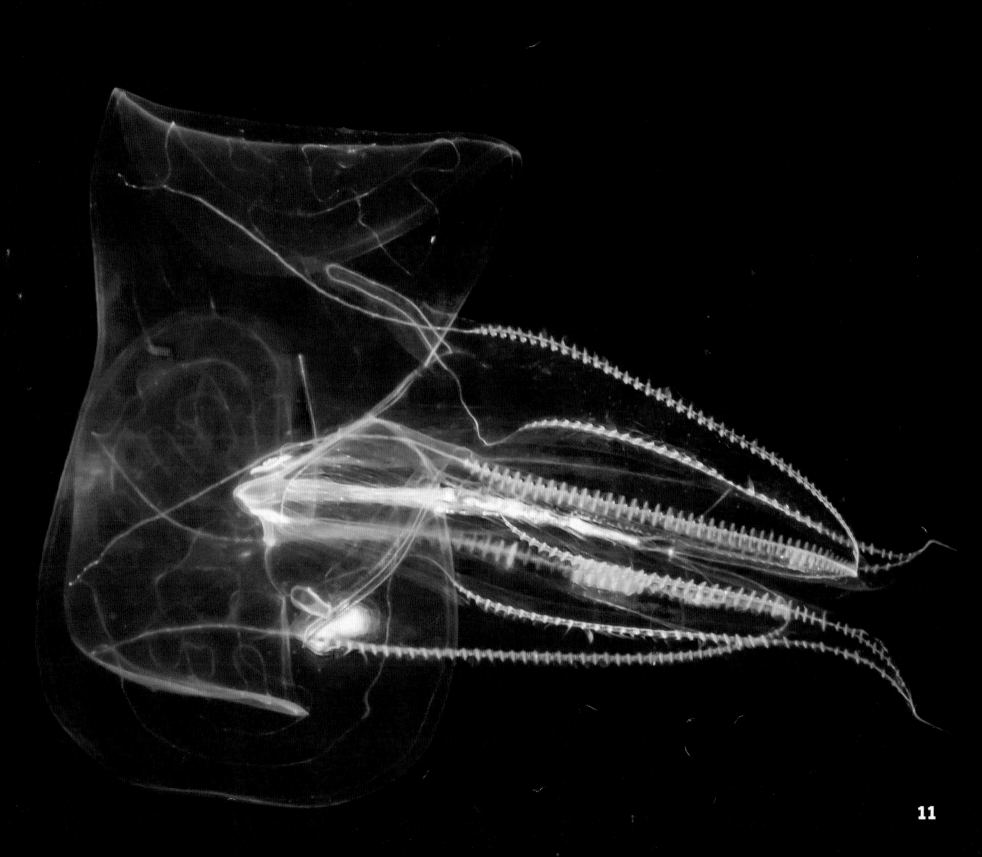

11

Jellyfish do not have bones.
They have soft bodies shaped
like bells or umbrellas.
They open and close their
bodies to move.

Finding food

Jellyfish have many tentacles. The tentacles sting prey with poison. Once they are stung, the prey cannot swim away.

The tentacles pull the prey
into the jellyfish's mouth.
Jellyfish eat fish and plankton.

Life cycle

Female jellyfish make eggs.
The eggs later grow into polyps.
Polyps live on the seabed.

19

Young jellyfish grow
from the polyps.
They break away and
move on their own.
In a few weeks, they
become adult jellyfish.

Glossary

plankton small or tiny animals and plants that drift or float in seas and oceans

poison substance that can kill or harm an animal or human

polyp jellyfish at the stage of development during which it lives on the seabed

prey animal hunted by another animal for food

tentacle long, flexible body part used for moving, feeling and grabbing

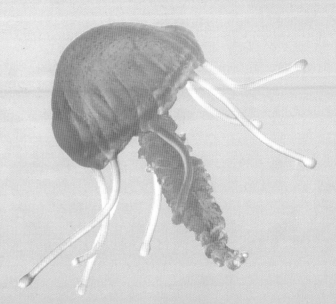

Read more

Jellyfish (A Day in the Life: Sea Animals), Louise Spilsbury (Raintree, 2011)

Sea Animals (Animals in their Habitats), Sian Smith (Raintree, 2014)

Usborne First Encyclopedia of Seas and Oceans, Jane Chisholm (Usborne Publishing, 2011)

Websites

www.bbc.co.uk/nature/life/Jellyfish
Watch videos and find out more about jellyfish.

www.national-aquarium.co.uk/50-fun-facts
Fun facts about sea and ocean life.

Index